PEARL

A NEW VERSE TRANSLATION

PEARL

= (middle English poem)

A NEW VERSE TRANSLATION

➤➤➤ ◀◀◀

by

MARIE BORROFF

YALE UNIVERSITY

W · W · Norton & Company · Inc · *New York*

FIRST EDITION

Grateful acknowledgment is made for permission to quote from
The Poems of Emily Dickinson, edited by Thomas H. Johnson
(Cambridge, The Belknap Press of Harvard University Press),
copyright 1951, 1955 by the President and Fellows of Harvard
College; and from "Stopping by Woods on a Snowy Evening,"
from *The Poetry of Robert Frost*, edited by Edward Connery
Lathem. Copyright 1923, 1969 by Holt, Rinehart & Winston;
copyright 1951 by Robert Frost. Reprinted by permission of Holt,
Rinehart & Winston, Publishers.

Library of Congress Cataloging in Publication Data
Pearl (Middle English poem)
   Pearl: a new verse translation.
   Bibliography: p.
   1. Borroff, Marie.
PR2111.A214   1977   821'.1   76–43971
          ISBN 0–393–04456–4 cloth edition
          ISBN 0–393–09144–9 paper edition

1 2 3 4 5 6 7 8 9 0

Contents

Introduction

Pearl (as modern editors have called it) is the first of four poems which make up the contents of a late fourteenth-century manuscript and are found only there. The manuscript seems to have been copied in the west Midlands of England, about seventy miles north-west of London, and the poet himself presumably lived in that area at about that time, though the evidence indicates that the texts of the four poems as we have them are the work of a copyist and not the author's own transcriptions. The words he wrote are neverthe-less well preserved, and that is fortunate, for all the poems are of great interest, and two of them—*Pearl* and *Sir Gawain and the Green Knight*—are acknowledged masterpieces.

Thematic Links with
Purity, Patience, and *Gawain*

We do not, of course, know for a fact that one poet wrote these four poems. If we think he did, it is not because they are written in the same language and reflect the same literary and cultural tradi-tions, but because they seem, at the deepest, most intimately sensed level of meaning, to be the work of one man's imagination. Who-ever and whatever this man was, he was a devout Christian at a time when the Christian church was also the Catholic Church. *Pearl* is a poem of doctrinal instruction in time of bereavement. The second poem in the manuscript, called *Purity,* begins by commend-ing the virtue described in the sixth Beatitude, "Blessed are the pure in heart, for they shall see God." Using the technique, common in medieval sermons, of illustrative narration, the poet tells a number of Old Testament stories showing that God is made angrier by impurity than by any other sin. The third poem, called *Patience,* commends in similar fashion the virtue described in the seventh Beatitude, which in the Latin Bible the poet would have known reads, "Blessed are they who suffer (*patiuntur*) persecution." The poet shows that it is best to bear patiently the hardships decreed by divine providence; he uses as his illustration the story of Jonah, who was punished for his obstinate refusal to do God's bidding by his sojourn in the whale, and rebuked by God for his impatience with the penitent citizens of Niniveh. *Sir Gawain and the Green Knight* is an Arthurian romance of adventure and enchantment, but its story, like the Arthurian legends generally, takes place in a Christian world and has its meaning in that world. Gawain himself interprets the humiliation that befalls him at the end of the poem as a punishment for covetousness brought on by cowardice, and covetousness (Latin *cupiditas*, or cupidity) in Christian tradition is that attachment to worldly things from which all other sins proceed. In the final episode, Sir Gawain makes a "confession," though not in a real church, and is "absolved," though not by a real priest. At the end of *Pearl*, the narrator, bemoaning his expulsion from the heavenly realm of his dream-vision, states an explicit moral:

> Had I but sought to content my Lord
> And taken his gifts without regret, . . .
> Drawn heavenward by divine accord
> I had seen and heard more mysteries yet;
> But always men would have and hoard
> And gain the more, the more they get.
> So banished I was, by cares beset,
> From realms eternal untimely sent;
> How madly, Lord, they strive and fret
> Whose acts accord not with your content!   XX,4*

The themes of impatience and covetousness link *Pearl* with *Patience* and *Sir Gawain*; it is linked with *Purity* by the recurrent theme of spotlessness or immaculateness, introduced in connection with the description of the narrator's lost pearl in the first section.

The Story

The story of the poem, on its most literal level, is easy to follow. As it opens, the narrator mourns a pearl of supreme value, and we soon realize that the terms in which he is describing it apply not only to a precious gem, but to a girl. His "secret pearl" has slipped from him into the ground; sweet herbs and spice plants have sprung up where it is buried. The bereaved man visits the spice garden, where he gives way to inconsolable grief and at last falls into a deep swoon. As his body lies asleep, his soul is transported to a resplendent landscape of unearthly beauty. Here he wanders about, his grief forgotten, but soon his way is blocked by a river which he wants above all else to cross, for the country beyond it is even more lovely than that on the nearer side—Paradise, he thinks, must surely be there. As he searches for a ford, he sees on the other side of the river a being who is at once a "child" and a "maiden" of stately bearing, dressed in royal robes and wearing a magnificent crown. Her dress is wholly white, adorned with many pearls; a single pearl

* Roman numerals refer to sections, and Arabic numerals to stanzas within sections, throughout.

of great price lies upon her breast. The sight of her stabs his heart, for he recognizes her as one he once knew well, who was "nearer to him than aunt or niece." The apparition comes down the shore on the other side of the river and greets him graciously. He hails her in return as his lost lamented pearl, but then elicits from her the first of a series of rebukes by complaining that she, lost to him, dwells in bliss while he is left to mourn.

This speech, and the pearl-maiden's answer, initiate a conversation between the two that takes up most of the rest of the poem. We know the narrator to be a Christian; even in his grief at the outset, he expresses his awareness of the "nature of Christ" and the comfort that is, at least theoretically, to be derived from it. But his knowledge of doctrine seems not to be matched by understanding, and the pearl-maiden must dispel a number of misapprehensions on his part. He cannot understand why he may not cross the stream and join her in blessedness forthwith. He does not see how she can be a queen in heaven when that rank is held by Mary; no one could take Mary's crown from her who did not surpass her in some respect, yet Mary is "singular," peerless, like the Phoenix. He finds it unjust that royal rank should have been bestowed on one whose accomplishments in life were negligible, who did not live two years on earth and could not even say her prayers or recite the creed. To resolve this last difficulty, the pearl-maiden tells him the New Testament parable of the vineyard (Matthew 20), according to which the owner of the vineyard pays each laborer the same wage, a single penny, for his day's work, no matter how late the hour at which it began; the owner of the vineyard stands for God, and the "penny" is eternal life in the heavenly kingdom. But this in turn baffles the dreamer. The equal wage is unreasonable, he says, and what is more, it contradicts a statement in the Bible which he can quote, that God "renders unto every man according to his work" (Psalms 62 [61]: 12).

At this point (and it is also the halfway point of the poem), the pearl-maiden's exposition shifts its emphasis from justice and right to grace and mercy. All men, as a result of Adam's disobedience to God, are born in sin, condemned to physical death and then to the second death of everlasting damnation. But Adam's guilt was redeemed by the voluntary death of Christ, which also expressed God's boundless love for mankind. The blood that ran from the pierced side of Christ on the cross symbolizes redemption, and the water that came with it signifies the sacrament of baptism, administered by the church, which brings redemption to the individual soul. A baptized child who dies in infancy has, it is true, done no works of righteousness, but neither has it sinned, whereas the best of men sin constantly and must repeatedly be returned to a state of grace through contrition and penance. The dead infant is an "innocent"—literally, one who has done no harm; the claim of such spotless souls to the bliss of heaven is wholly in accord with reason, and indeed is clearer than that of the righteous man.

The pearl-maiden has spoken sternly, and she has matched the dreamer's quotation from the Psalms with another, more threatening one, to the effect that no man shall be justified in the sight of the Lord (143 [142]: 2). Her tone now changes as she speaks of the tenderness of the living Jesus, who invited the little children to come to him. The figure of the child unspotted by sin knocking at the gate of the kingdom of heaven, which will open straightway to receive him, opens a new phase in the development of the poem in which materials from the Old Testament, the Gospels, and the Book of Revelation, as interpreted in early church tradition, are woven together in language of unsurpassed intensity and power. The pearl now enters for the first time in its major symbolic role as the "one pearl of great price" in the parable told by Jesus in the Gospel of Matthew, for which the merchant seeking goodly pearls sold all he had. The maiden explains that the pearl is like the heavenly kingdom; it is spotless, like the souls of the innocent; it is perfectly round and thus "endless," like eternity; it is "blithe" and thus represents the bliss of the redeemed. This pearl of great price is, in fact, the "one pure pearl" visible upon the maiden's breast, bestowed upon her by the Lamb at the time of their wedding in token of the peace of heaven and the spotlessness for which he loved her.

Just as the dreamer had supposed that there could be only one queen in heaven, so he now supposes that the pearl-maiden, in becoming the bride of the Lamb, must have been preferred to all others, including many women who had lived and died for Christ in saintly fashion. But the maiden, carefully distinguishing between two similar words in Middle English, explains that while she is indeed spotless (*maskeles*, or immaculate), she is not unique (*makeles*, or matchless). She reveals herself to be one of the 144,000 virgins seen with the Lamb on Mount Sion in the New Jerusalem by St. John the Divine, and described by him in the Book of Revelation. These in turn were identified in medieval tradition with the Holy Innocents whose martyrdom is celebrated yearly by the church—the children under the age of two whom Herod killed, thinking thus to kill the infant Jesus. The pearl-maiden, who did not live two years on earth, has joined this celestial company. The bridegroom to whom all of them alike are wedded, and with whom they live in joy, is the Lamb of God, invoked by Isaiah in the Old Testament as he that takes away the sins of the world, condemned to death by the Jews in Jerusalem and crucified there, and seen in heaven beside the throne of God by St. John the Divine.

This exposition gives rise to another misunderstanding on the dreamer's part. The pearl-maiden has told him that she lives with the Lamb, but that cannot be in "Jerusalem," for she is there on the other side of the river and Jerusalem is on earth, in the kingdom of Judea. This confusion in turn is resolved by the maiden, who distinguishes between the Old Jerusalem, where the trial and crucifixion of Christ took place, and the New Jerusalem, seen descending out of heaven by St. John (Revelation 21). In accordance with the traditional interpretations of the name *Jerusalem* as "city of God" and "sight of peace," this latter is the city where the souls of the blessed, once their bodies have suffered earthly death and decay, dwell with God in eternal harmony and rest.

The request the dreamer now makes, as he speaks for the last time, poignantly reflects his love for the maiden in her former condition as a human child. He wants, he says, to see the place where she lives, the great city and the "blissful bower," the wedding chamber, within it. Here, late in the unfoldment of the narrative as also in *Sir Gawain and the Green Knight*, we learn what has set the entire sequence of events in motion, beginning with the narrator's swoon over the mound in the herb garden. The pearl-maiden tells him that no mortal may enter the celestial city, but that "through great favor" she has obtained permission from the Lamb for him to see it from the outside. She has, that is, interceded for him that he may be brought out of his spiritual impasse, mediating between him and God as the saints, when men pray to them, are thought to do. Beneath her seemingly impersonal, if not cold, attitude toward him during much of their conversation lies the loving concern implicit in this act.

The description of the celestial Jerusalem, seen by the dreamer across the river from a hill to which the pearl-maiden has directed him, follows closely—much of the time almost word for word—the description in the Book of Revelation, as if the poet wished thereby to insist on the authenticity of the vision. There are the twelve foundations, each made of a single precious stone; the cubic shape as St. John saw it measured; the twelve pearly gates; the golden streets; and, within the city, the throne of God and the elders seated about it. Then, as, on earth, the risen full moon begins to shine in the east while it is still daylight (such is the poem's unforgettable simile), the dreamer becomes aware of a procession moving toward the throne, led by the Lamb and made up of the thousands upon thousands of his brides. All are dressed as the pearl-maiden had been dressed, all wear the pearl of great price. In a moment of all but unbearable poignancy, he sees among the others in the procession his "little queen." As he recognizes her, the entrancement of spiritual vision gives way to that delight in the sight of the beloved which for earthly beings is inseparable from the desire to possess. He rushes toward the river, determined to cross it, come what may, and wakens from his dream.

Symbolism and Theme

Such is the density of symbolic meaning in *Pearl* that the story of the poem, maiden and all, has sometimes been interpreted wholly in allegorical terms. But the force of certain details seems clearly circumstantial, pointing toward the story of an individual man as much as to that of the Christian soul in general, and the common-sense view has prevailed in more recent criticism: that the poem is at once autobiographical and allegorical, founded on an actual experience of bereavement and dealing with that experience in terms of Christian symbols and doctrine.

Another question of interpretation has to do with the so-called obtuseness of the dreamer. It is implausible (the argument runs) that he, a professed Christian, should not already understand the doctrinal points the maiden is making, should keep asking virtually the same question again and again. But his persistent wrongheaded-ness makes sense if we consider how deeply founded it is in the limitations of the mortal perspective. Seeing the pearl-maiden standing on the other side of a river, he naturally concludes that she is "there" in the same sense in which another person would be there, a certain distance away, in life. Actually, the dreamed encounter by the river, within speaking range, symbolizes the maiden's role as an intermediary between the dreamer and the heavenly realm to which he does not belong. Even as the maiden speaks to him, one is tempted to say, she is in the procession moving through the streets of the celestial Jerusalem in the company of the Lamb, as the dreamer sees her to be at the end of the poem. Yet the processional itself, like the marriage relationship, is a symbol of spiritual union, the visible for the invisible. Such questions as "Where is she really?" "What is she really doing?" have no answer, indeed no meaning, on this plane.

So too with the pearl. At the beginning of the poem, it stands for what has been most precious to the narrator in this world—in Shakespeare's words, there where he has garnered up his heart. Seeing the maiden, recognizing her (so it seems) as the very being he so loves, the dreamer naturally thinks that what he has found is what he had lost. He does not and at this stage cannot realize that his earthly pearl has passed into another mode of existence. All that was truly precious in her is now forever merged in the transcendent values of the heavenly kingdom. She can be possessed only by possessing that, and that can be possessed only by giving up the things of this world, as the merchant sold all he had to obtain the one pearl of the parable.

But between earthly and divine orders there is a separation which cannot be bridged by the unaided efforts of the human mind. The characteristics of the pearl as the maiden describes them in telling the parable of the merchant are signs of this radical discontinuity. Having the form of a circle, the pearl, as we have already observed, stands for eternity, the existence of God in a timeless present from the perspective of which human history is a completed, static pattern. Human beings are trapped in progressive time, looking back from the present to the past and forward to an unknown future. Eternity is not perpetual duration, "longer than" time; it is the absence of time. So too with the worth of the heavenly pearl. It is not "greater than" the worth of anything on earth; it is absolute, literally "beyond measure." Nearer and farther, earlier and later, lower and higher, less and more, all are interdependent manifestations of a dimensional mode of being in which men, under the governance of changing fortune, move toward certain death. "We look before and after, And pine for what is not": the inner dissatisfaction and perpetual striving inevitable in such a world have their otherworldly counterparts in the peace of heaven. To dwell there is to possess a happiness which, again, is not "greater than" human happiness, but perfect, without qualification.

From this disparity arise all the paradoxes and contradictions which baffle the dreamer so. That everyone in heaven is a king or queen; that the "penny" of eternal life, the wage of everyone who works in the vineyard, has no relation to comparative deserts; that everyone in heaven has the same reward "no matter how little or great his gains" (XI, 1)—such statements cannot be understood in common-sense, "realistic" terms. They are attempts to express in language what language was not designed to express.

The dreamer, for all that he is transported to a "place" of visionary enlightenment, cannot escape the habit of insatiable desire emphasized as thematic by the poet's choice of *more* as link-word in sections III and X, and by the complementary choice of *nevertheless* in section XV. Yet the experience of the dream does change him, and the evolution of his attitudes and feelings in the course of the poem breathes dramatic life into what would otherwise have been unrelieved didacticism. At first, as we saw, he is querulous and self-centered, then brash and presumptuous in assuming that he and the glorious personage on the other side of the river exist on the same plane. For this latter misapprehension he receives her coldest rebuke. But then he takes an important step: forsaking his obstinacy and confessing his foolishness, he throws himself on God's mercy in a kind of self-administered baptism (VII, 1):

> As water flows from a fountainhead
> I cast myself in his mercy clear.

More important, he stops thinking solely about what he has suffered and what he desires, and begins to sense his own ignorance about what it is he is seeing. The question he asks, "What is your life?" (VII, 3), has, at the moment of asking, profounder implications than he or we realize. The answer, it turns out, is life itself—in Christian terms, that life compared to which what is called "life" on earth is a continual dying. By the time the maiden has expounded the parable of the vineyard and justified the place in heaven of the innocent, the dreamer is filled with awe, overwhelmed by her angelic aspect and more than earthly magnificence even as he remains still wrongheaded, still trying to understand her heavenly station in terms of what he knows. His last request is made with the utmost reverence and humility, though it too is humanly motivated, reflecting the same partiality which leads at last to his ill-fated attempt to cross the river.

What, in the end, has he learned? We have already heard his self-admonishment in the concluding section. If, he thinks, he had been less impatient, more willing to be content with what had been granted him, he would not have been banished so soon from the country of his vision. But this facile moralizing hardly addresses the problem of his initial despair, and a far deeper lesson is implicit in the terms of his farewell to the pearl-maiden.

> Then sorrow broke from my burning breast;
> "O honored Pearl," I said, "how dear
> Was your every word and wise behest
> In this true vision vouchsafed me here.
> If you in a garland never sere
> Are set by that Prince all-provident,
> Then happy am I in dungeon drear
> That he with you is well content."

In the symbol of the garland, a completed circle, we see an intimation of eternity on the speaker's part. The disparity between garland and dungeon further suggests his realization that the mortal and immortal realms are closed off from each other, that the "distance" between the two cannot be crossed as if it were a river. It is significant that nowhere in the final stanzas does he speak of his hope to be reunited with his pearl in heaven, or of his anticipation of that reunion, in expressing his reconcilement to his earthly lot. The deepest lesson he has been taught is an imaginative apprehension of what his lost pearl now is, part of an everlasting and changeless order. Such a garland, unlike one made of earthly flowers, cannot fade, nor can the man lose it who has learned to value it properly.

Knowing this, and grateful for the grace that has accorded him the enlightening vision, the speaker commits to God his pearl and his poem, calling down upon both the blessing of Christ and praying that all men may be made conformable to the divine willl.

The Literary Background

We have so far seen *Pearl* exclusively in relation to the Bible and Christian tradition. But it is an imaginative, as well as a doctrinal, work, and we must therefore say something about its literary background as well. Knowing little or nothing about the author's life, we cannot attempt a full account of influences and sources as we might for a Yeats or a Stevens. But it is obvious that *Pearl* shares important elements of theme and dramatic presentation with two major literary works which were so widely read in the Middle Ages that the poet would inevitably have known them: *The Consolation of Philosophy* and *The Romance of the Rose*.

The Consolation of Philosophy, like *Pearl*, has its point of departure in the circumstances and mental state of its narrator. Boethius, who lived in the late fifth and early sixth centuries, was thrown into prison and finally executed after having enjoyed prosperity and power under the Roman emperor Theodoric. At the beginning of the *Consolation* he speaks as a captive, complaining of the conditions in which he finds himself, unable to reconcile himself to the loss of his former good fortune. He is visited by a feminine being of supernatural majesty whom he belatedly recognizes as Philosophy, the "nurse of his youth." There follows a lengthy conversation between the two in which the prisoner's role is largely passive. Philosophy rebukes him for his despair, and consoles him by gradually leading him to a full understanding of the relationship between transitory and lasting goods. The former are the gifts to men on earth of the changeable goddess Fortuna, who will inevitably take them away. The latter belong to man's soul, which is also his rational intelligence; once possessed, they cannot be lost.

The lesson of the *Consolation*, though it is presented in philosophic rather than religious terms, is much the same as what I have described as the implicit lesson of *Pearl*. But if the "meaning" of *Pearl* is to this extent Boethian, the emotional climate of the poem is far otherwise. *Pearl* is not only a dialogue affording doctrinal enlightenment, it is a dream-vision suffused with the ardor of what we now call romantic love. In this it resembles that greatest exemplar of the medieval dream-vision, *The Romance of the Rose*, a poem we know the *Pearl*-poet had read and admired because he alludes to it in *Purity*. Written in the first half of the thirteenth century by the French poet Guillaume de Lorris, the first part of the

Romance describes a wonderful dream which begins on a May morning. The youthful narrator (he is, he tells us, at the age when love rules men's hearts) finds himself in a delightful landscape which shares with the dream landscape of *Pearl* such features as leafy trees and bushes and joyfully singing birds, though these are more naturalistically described. Wandering about, delighting in the beauty of the scene, he pauses to bathe his face in a clear stream, then follows along its bank. At last he comes to a garden or park surrounded by a high wall, to which he succeeds in gaining access. Neither the garden nor its inhabitants, chief among whom is the god of love, need be described here; more important with relation to *Pearl* is the dreamer's discovery, within the garden, of a fountain at the bottom of which are two brilliant crystal stones. He gazes into the fountain and sees reflected there a bush laden with blooming red roses to which he is immediately attracted. Seen close at hand, it enraptures him with its sweetness, and one especially beautiful rose-bud becomes the object of his love. The story that follows tells of his frustrated attempts to gain possession of the rose, but de Lorris did not complete the poem, and it was continued in more satiric and discursive vein by Jean de Meun.

The Romance of the Rose is an allegory of love on the human plane. But the conventional language of secular love poetry in medieval times was also used in a considerable body of religious poetry addressed to the Virgin Mary. In *Pearl*, the feelings of a father for his lost infant daughter, who appears to him as an angelic visitant, are expressed in this same language. As has often been noted, the maiden has the typical physical attributes of the idealized mistress—slender figure, grey eyes, hair like gold, flawless complexion—and the terms in which the dreamer addresses her—"my jewel," "my sweet," "my adored one"—are such as a lover would use to his lady. Yet she is also a virgin and a saint, and other terms applied to her—"special spice," "immaculate bride," "immaculate maid so meek and mild"—clearly associate her with Mary. The educational process dramatized in *Pearl* involves, not the negation of human passion, but its removal from the realm of mutability—a lifting up of the heart to higher things.

Design and Its Significance

One of the most striking and significant aspects of the poem is its conformity to an all-encompassing and highly elaborated design. Elements of this design are found separately elsewhere, but the intricacy of their combination in *Pearl* is unmatched in English poetry before or since. The twelve-line stanza used by the poet is found in many other Middle English poems on religious subjects;

the stanzas of these poems characteristically end in a repeated or varied refrain. The rhyme scheme, abababbcbc, is an extraordinarily difficult one. It requires no fewer than four a-rhymes and six b-rhymes per stanza, and the repetition of the refrain calls for a number of c-rhymes as well. *Pearl* is divided into twenty sections, each of which, with the exception of section XV, contains five stanzas. The last line of each of the five stanzas making up a given section ends in a link-word which is sometimes part of a repeated phrase ("without a spot," "is enough for all"); the same link-word also appears in the first lines of all but one of the five stanzas. The sections themselves are joined by the device of "concatenation," or overlapping repetition: the link-word of a given section appears in the first line of the first stanza of the following section. For example, in the last stanza of section III, the link-word *more* appears in the first and last lines; it makes its final appearance in the first line of the first stanza of section IV, which ends with the new linking phrase "pearls of price":

> The more I mused on that fair face,
> The person of that most precious one,
> Such gladness grew in my heart by grace
> As little before had been, or none.
> I longed to call across that space
> But found my powers of speech had flown;
> To meet her in so strange a place—
> Such a sight, in truth, might shock or stun!
> Then raised she up her brow, that shone
> All ivory pale on that far shore,
> That stabbed my heart to look upon
> And ever the longer, more and more.
>
> More dread diminished my delight;
> I stood stock-still and dared not call.
> With eyes wide open and mouth shut tight
> I hoved there tame as hawk in hall.
> Unearthly, I knew, must be that plight;
> I dreaded much what might befall,
> Lest she I viewed should vanish quite
> And leave me there to stare and stall.
> That slender one, so smooth, so small,
> Unblemished, void of every vice,
> Rose up in robes imperial,
> A precious pearl in pearls of price.

Finally, it is important to note that the link-word of the final section also appears, in rhyming position, in the first line of the first stanza of the poem. The end is thus connected back to the beginning in a kind of temporal circularity. The presence of the statement "I am alpha and omega, the first and the last," in chapters 1 and 22 of the Book of Revelation has been thought to be an instance of this same device. A modern example of both circularity and concatenation is Donne's "La Corona" (The Crown), in which each of seven sonnets has as its first line the last line of the preceding one, and the last line of the last is also the first line of the first. The thematic significance of such a pattern in a poem so entitled need scarcely be pointed out, and we are reminded that circularity is also a symbolic attribute of the pearl.

Circularity or roundness is a symbol not only of eternity, but of perfection: Philosophy, in the *Consolation,* quotes the ancient philosopher Parmenides to the effect that "the divine essence is 'in body like a sphere, perfectly rounded on all sides.' " Another visible symbol of perfection is symmetry, exemplified most notably in *Pearl* in the shape of the celestial Jerusalem. The poet repeats the description given by St. John, who saw the city measured; it was 12,000 furlongs in length, breadth, and height, a perfect cube. Symmetry is further exemplified by the outer walls of the city, each with its three gates. The number twelve is the total number of gates, the number of the trees growing beside the river of life, and the base of the city's measurement in furlongs. It is also the number of lines in the stanzas of *Pearl.* The square of a number is a mathematical expression of symmetry, and the square of twelve, multiplied by a thousand, is the number of the virgins accompanying the Lamb. Given these facts, we cannot fail to find it significant that the one hundred and one stanzas of *Pearl* have a total of 1212 lines. But one hundred is also the square of the "perfect number," ten, in which the decimal sequence returns to one plus zero, and the one-hundred-and-first stanza of the poem can be thought of as overlapping, and thus coinciding with, the first stanza, to close the circle. Corroborating evidence of the *Pearl*-poet's interest in number and numerical design is found in *Sir Gawain and the Green Knight.* The last alliterating line of this poem echoes its first, the essential action begins and ends on New Year's Day, and there is a lengthy explanation of the significance of the number five in Gawain's emblem, the pentangle, or five-pointed star, which, because it is drawn in one continuous line ending where it began, is called "the endless knot." Finally, it is a curious fact that in *Gawain,* as in *Pearl,* the total number of stanzas is one hundred and one.

It is natural for the modern reader to wonder whether all this patterning in *Pearl* is mere display—artifice for artifice's sake. But the very question implies that the answer may be found in the relationship between display and purpose, form and content, or, to use a characteristically medieval analogy often applied to literary works, husk and kernel. Most obviously in the realm of tangible artifacts, painstaking elaboration signifies and confers value. In early times, the hand-copied manuscript was such an artifact; we think of the gorgeously bound and illuminated Bibles, missals, and books of hours whose material worth was a sign that they bore a priceless message. We think too of the medieval reliquary with its profusion of ornament worked in ivory or metal. And these in turn suggest an important group of images in *Pearl*: the jeweler, the jewel, and the enclosing box. The dreamer in section V tells the maiden that since he has been separated from her he has been "a joyless jeweler"; the maiden replies that he is mistaken—his pearl cannot be lost to him when it is enclosed in so comely a "coffer" as the garden in which he sees her. There is a grim pun here, for *coffer* in Middle English could also mean "coffin" (I have substituted *casket*, which has a similar mortuary meaning in American English). The root-meaning of the word *garden* is in fact "enclosed place"; the garden of Eden where Adam and Eve first lived was a bounded precinct, a kind of park. Heaven was commonly visualized as a celestial version of the earthly paradise. Alternatively, it was visualized as a city, the celestial Jerusalem. This latter, having walls, is also a kind of enclosure or box—a coffer, fashioned sumptuously of precious substances, containing the treasure of eternal life. An analogy becomes irresistible: the verbal artifact called *Pearl* is itself a kind of painstakingly crafted container, embellished with every device of language in order that it may be worthy of its contents, the vision of the pearl-maiden and the precious teachings she imparts.

Design in *Pearl* has an additional dimension of significance. Like any literary work, the poem exists temporally rather than spatially; it must be experienced part by part. But having been experienced, it can be contemplated, in terms of its numerical form, its sections, its stanzas, its rhymes, and its metrical patterns, as a patterned object. Moving through time toward a condition of timelessness, the poem embodies the aspiration it dramatically represents.

The Translation

In translating *Pearl*, I have reproduced the schemes of rhyme, repetition, and concatenation described above; whatever difficulties these present, the poem could scarcely retain its identity without them. I have also followed the poet as best I could in the linking of stressed syllables by initial alliteration, especially in passages of heightened dramatic intensity. Language in these latter is at times loaded with alliteration, consonance, and other linkages among sounds to the point where the shapes of words threaten to become more conspicuous than their sense, and similar effects have found their way into my translation. Lines such as

> His gifts gush forth like a spring in spate
> Or a stream in a gulley that runs in rains,

or

> As in his flock no fleck is seen,
> His hallowed halls are wholly bright,

may strike the modern reader as overwrought, but they have their counterparts in the poem, and would not, I think, have offended the ears to which it was first addressed.

Another kind of verbal extravagance in which *Pearl* abounds is word-play. The necessity of repeating the link-words leads to the sort of pun that exploits the range of senses of a single word, as when *spot* means both "speck" and "place," *deem* both "express an opinion" and "pronounce sentence," and *right* both "valid claim" and "rectitude." But the *Pearl*-poet did not eschew the lowliest form of wit either. He substitutes *now* for the link-word *enow* "enough" in XI, 2, and in section XVI uses two words of identical form, *mote* "speck" and *mote* "walled city" (related to *moat*). (Elsewhere in the poem he puns on yet another word spelled *mote*, modern *moot*, meaning "debate" or "strife.") He seems to rejoice in the phonetic identity in his dialect of *lamb* and *lamp*, writing "God himself was their lamp-light [the text has the spelling *lombe-lyght*], The Lamb their lantern" (XVIII, 2). These homonymic puns cannot be reproduced in modern English, but in view of their presence in the original, I have felt justified in combining *wholly* and *holy* as link-word in section XVI—a pun which is in fact of the more respectable sort, since the two words go back to a single root.

As for the diction of the translation, I have tried to conform to the original in making it at once traditional and varied. It would not have occurred to the author of *Pearl* to avoid formulaic combinations of words, whether poetic or colloquial, or to think of such combinations as "clichés" in the modern derogatory sense. I have made use of some distinctively literary diction, as the *Pearl*-poet himself did, though I have tried to avoid burned-out archaisms. The occasional echo of Milton, Shakespeare, or the King James Bible, when it suggested itself, was allowed to stay, and stock phrases like "heart's desire," "daily round," "lost and lamented," "royal road," and others, have been incorporated as in keeping with the poet's own style. I have also emulated a complementary effect of diction in *Pearl*, of the deployment or display of abundant resources. One has the impression that the poet never inadvertently repeats an adjective, a rhyming combination, or even a rhyme sound. Important attributes such as spotlessness, brightness, and happiness seem to be described in endlessly fresh combinations of words, and this aspect of the language offers a particular challenge to the translator, as well as conferring on the poem a richness befitting its character as an artifact.

In *Pearl*, if in any poem, we see the poet offering up his craft, creating expressive power out of the very restrictions imposed upon expression. To emulate such an achievement is an act of the greatest temerity, especially since, as with dancing on pointe, the limitations accepted by the artist are justified only insofar as he transcends them. The result of my long labors may or may not be found worthy of comparison with the original; "if not," in the words of Emily Dickinson,

I had
The transport of the aim.

New Haven, Connecticut   Marie Borroff
March, 1976

Acknowledgments

I am grateful to E. Talbot Donaldson, who believed in the possibility of this translation; to my colleagues John Freccero, A. Bartlett Giamatti, and Dorothee Metlitski for helpful discussion and moral support; and to Robert B. Burlin for sharing with me his work on *Pearl*. I was fortunate to have the assistance in research of M. Teresa Tavormina, who brought to my attention the late medieval bridal crown used in the jacket design of this book. The passage from author's copy to finished manuscript was made smooth by the unfailing interest and expertise of Mrs. Doris Nelson.

John C. Pope was the tutelary spirit of the enterprise from the outset, and the work benefited at every stage from his suggestions. I owe a special debt to Sherry Reames for the thoroughgoing criticism, laced with encouragement, which gave me a needed impetus in the eleventh hour.

MARIE BORROFF

PEARL

A NEW VERSE TRANSLATION

Pearl

I

1

Pearl, that a prince is well content
To give a circle of gold to wear,
Boldly I say, all orient
Brought forth none precious like to her;
So comely in every ornament,
So slender her sides, so smooth they were,
Ever my mind was bound and bent
To set her apart without a peer.
In a garden of herbs I lost my dear;
Through grass to ground away it shot;
Now, lovesick, the heavy loss I bear
Of that secret pearl without a spot.

2

Since in that spot it sped from me so,
Often I watched and wished for that grace
That once was wont to banish woe
And bless with brightness all my days;
That clutches my heart in cruel throe
And causes my blood to rage and race,
Yet sweeter songs could no man know
Than silence taught my ear to trace;
And many there came, to think of her face
With cover of clay so coldly fraught:
O earth, you mar a gem past praise,
My secret pearl without a spot.

3

That spot with spice must spring and spread
Where riches rotted in narrow room;
Blossoms white and blue and red
Lift now alight in blaze of noon;
Flower and fruit could never fade
Where pearl plunged deep in earthen tomb,
For the seed must die to bear the blade
That the wheat may be brought to harvest home.[1]
Good out of good to all and some:
Such a seed could never have come to nought
Nor spice in splendor spare to bloom
From that precious pearl without a spot.

1. John 12:24.

4

To that especial spot I hied
And entered that same garden green
In August at a festive tide
When corn is cut with scythe-edge keen.
On the mound where pearl went tumbling wide,
Leaf vied with leaf in shade and sheen:
Gillyflower and ginger on every side
And peonies peerless blooming between.
But fairer yet, and all unseen,
Was the fragrance that my senses sought;
There, I know, is the dear demesne
Of my precious pearl without a spot.

5

Before that spot with head inclined
I stretched my hand in stark despair;
My heart lamented, deaf and blind,
Though reason reconciled my care.
I mourned my pearl so close confined
With thoughts in throng contending there;
Comfort of Christ might come to mind
But wretched will would not forbear.
I fell upon that flower-bed fair;
Such odor seized my brain distraught
I slipped into slumber unaware,
On that precious pearl without a spot.

II

1

My soul forsook that spot in space
And left my body on earth to bide.
My spirit sped, by God's good grace,
On a quest where marvels multiplied.
I knew not where in the world it was,
But I saw I was set where cliffs divide;
A forest flourished in that place
Where many rich rocks might be descried.
The glory that flashed there far and wide
Eye could not credit, nor mind invent;
Pure cloth-of-gold were pale beside
Such rich and rare embellishment.

2

Embellished were those hills in view
With crystal cliffs as clear as day
And groves of trees with boles as blue

As indigo silks of rich assay;
The leaves, like silver burnished new,
Slide rustling rife on every spray;
As shifts of cloud let sunshine through,
They shot forth light in shimmering play.
The gravelstones that strewed the way
Were precious pearls of orient;
The beams of the sun but blind and grey
Beside such bright embellishment.

3

Amid those hills embellished bright
My sorrows fled in full retreat;
Fragrance of fruits with great delight
Filled me like food that mortals eat.
Birds of all colors fanned in flight
Their iridescent pinions fleet,
But lute or lyre, by craft or sleight,
Could not make music half so sweet,
For while in time their wings they beat
In glad accord their voices blent;
With more of mirth might no man meet
Than hear each brave embellishment.

4

So all embellished was the land
Where Fortune bears me on my way;
No tongue is worthy to command
Fit words those splendors to display.
I walked along with bliss at hand;
No slope so steep to make me stay;
The further, the fairer the pear trees stand,
The spice-plants spread, the blossoms sway,
And hedgerows run by banks as gay
As glittering golden filament;
I came to the shore of a waterway:
Dear God, what brave embellishment!

5

Embellishing those waters deep,
Banks of pure beryl greet my gaze;
Sweetly the eddies swirl and sweep
With a rest and a rush in murmuring phrase;
Stones in the stream their colors steep,
Gleaming like glass where sunbeam strays,
As stars, while men of the marshlands sleep,
Flash in winter from frosty space;
For every one was a gem to praise,
A sapphire or emerald opulent,

That seemed to set the pool ablaze,
So brilliant their embellishment.

III

1

Embellished with such wondrous grace
Were wood and water and shining plain,
My pleasures multiplied apace,
Conquered my cares, dispelled my pain.
By the brink of a river that runs a race
Blissful I walked with busy brain;
The more I explored that plashy place
The greater strength did gladness gain.
As proof of Fortune's purpose plain
Makes a man's heart to sink or soar,
He whom she plies with bliss or bane
Of what he draws is dealt still more.

2

More of bliss was there to prize
Than ever my tongue could testify,
For earthly heart could not suffice
To sustain one tenth of that pure joy.
It could not be but Paradise
Lay beyond those noble banks, thought I,
And the stream itself seemed a device,
A mark to know a boundary by.
Those peerless precincts to espy
I need but gain the further shore;
But I dared not wade, for the water ran high,
And longing mastered me more and more.

3

More than ever and ever the more
To cross that river was all my care,
For lovely though this landscape were,
What lay beyond was past compare.
I stared about, scanning the shore
For a ford to afford me thoroughfare,
But dangers direr than before
Appeared, the more I wandered there.
And still it seemed I should not forbear
For dangers, with delights in store;
But now was broached a new affair
My mind was moved by, more and more.

4

More marvels now amazed me quite:
Beyond that stream, strange to behold,

There rose a cliff of crystal bright
With resplendent rays all aureoled.
At the foot was seated in plain sight
A maiden child of mortal mold,
A gracious lady gowned in white;
I knew her well, I had seen her of old.
As fine-spun floss of burnished gold,
So shone she, peerless, as of yore;
I gazed on her with joy untold,
The longer, I knew her more and more.

5

The more I mused on that fair face,
The person of that most precious one,
Such gladness grew in my heart by grace
As little before had been, or none.
I longed to call across that space
But found my power of speech had flown;
To meet her in so strange a place—
Such a sight, in truth, might shock or stun!
Then raised she up her brow, that shone
All ivory pale on that far shore,
That stabbed my heart to look upon
And ever the longer, more and more.

IV

1

More dread diminished my delight;
I stood stock-still and dared not call.
With eyes wide open and mouth shut tight
I hoved there tame as hawk in hall.
Unearthly, I knew, must be that plight;
I dreaded much what might befall,
Lest she I viewed should vanish quite
And leave me there to stare and stall.
That slender one, so smooth, so small,
Unblemished, void of every vice,
Rose up in robes imperial,
A precious pearl in pearls of price.

2

Pearls of price in ample store
Were there to see by grace divine
As she, approaching, shone on shore
Like fleurs-de-lys to kings condign.
Her surcoat of white linen pure[2]
Had open sides of fair design,
And filigree on bands it bore

2. Revelation 19:7–8 (cf. VII, 5:5–6).

Where lavish pearls their lustre join,
And lappets large, with double line
Of pearls set round in that same guise;
Her gown of that same linen fine,
And all bedecked with pearls of price.

3

Her priceless crown with pearls alone
Was set, in fashion fit and fair;
High pinnacles upon it shone,
And florets carved with craft and care.
Other headdress had she none
To frame her ivory forehead bare;
As earl or duke by royal throne,
So sage she seemed, so grave her air.
About her shoulders fell her hair
Like gold spun fine by artifice,
Whose deepest hue yet had a share
Of pallor pure of pearls of price.

4

Pearls of price in rows ornate
On hem, on side, on wristband rest;
No other gem could suit her state
Who was in white so richly dressed.
But one pure pearl, a wonder great,
Was set secure upon her breast;
A man might ponder long and late
Ere its full worth were well assessed.
I think no tongue could ever attest
A discourteous thought of that device,
So white it was, so wholly blessed,
And proudest placed of pearls of price.

5

In pearls of price she moved at ease
Toward the rim of the river that flowed so free;
No gladder man from here to Greece
Than I, that blessèd sight to see.
She was nearer my heart than aunt or niece:
So much the more my joy must be;
She proffered parley in sign of peace,
Bowed womanlike with bended knee,
Took off her crown of high degree
And bade me welcome with courteous voice;
That I was born O well for me
To greet that girl in pearls of price.

V

1

"O pearl," said I, ' in pearls of price,
Are you my pearl come back again,
Lost and lamented with desolate sighs
In darkest night, alone and in vain?
Since you slipped to ground where grasses rise
I wander pensive, oppressed with pain,
And you in the bliss of Paradise,
Beyond all passion and strife and strain.
What fate removed you from earth's domain
And left me hapless and heartsick there?
Since parting was set between us twain
I have been a joyless jeweler."

2

That jewel then with fair gems fraught
Lifted her face with eyes of grey,
Set on her crown and stood in thought,
And soberly then I heard her say,
"Sir, your tale is told for nought,
To say your pearl has gone away
That is closed in a coffer so cunningly wrought
As this same garden green and gay,
And here forever in joy to stay
Where lack nor loss can never come near;
Here were a casket fit to display
A prize for a proper jeweler.

3

"But, jeweler, if your mind is bound
To mourn for a gem in solitude,
Your care has set you a course unsound,
And a cause of a moment maddens your mood;
You lost a rose that grew in the ground:
A flower that fails and is not renewed,
But such is the coffer closing it round,
With the worth of a pearl it is now imbued.
And fate, you say, has robbed you of good,
That rendered you profit free and clear;
You blame a blessing misunderstood:
You are no proper jeweler."

4

A jewel to me then was this guest
And jewels her gentle sayings were.
"O blissful one," I said, "and best,

You have healed me wholly of heartache here!
To be excused I make request:
My pearl was away, I knew not where;
Now I have found it, now I shall rest,
And live with it ever, and make good cheer,
And love the Lord and his laws revere
That brought me the blissful sight of her.
Let me once cross and behold you near,
And I am a joyful jeweler!"

5

"Jeweler," said that gem at this,
"Such mockery comes of mortal pride!
Most ill-advised your answer is
And errors grave your thoughts misguide.
Three statements you have made amiss;
Your words from your wit have wandered wide;
You think me set in this vale of bliss
For so you see me, the brook beside;
The second, you say you shall abide
With me in this far country here;
The third, to cross this deep divide,
Behooves no joyful jeweler.

VI

1

"I hold that jeweler little to praise
Who believes no more than meets the eye,
And little courtesy he displays
Who doubts the word of the Lord on high
That faithfully pledged your flesh to raise
Though Fortune made it fail and die;
They twist the sense of his words and ways
Who believe what they see, and else deny;
And that is pride and obstinacy
And ill accords with honest intent,
To think each tale must be a lie
Except his reason give assent.

2

"Say, do you not, dissenting, strive
Against God's will that all should uphold?
Here in this land you mean to live—
You might ask leave to make so bold!
Nor can you with such ease contrive
To cross this water deep and cold;
Your body fair, with senses five,
Must first sink down in mire and mold,

For in Eden garden, in days of old,
Our fathers' father his life misspent;
Each man must suffer a death foretold
Ere God to this crossing give consent."

3

"Consent," said I, "to that hard fate
And you have cleft my heart in twain.
That which I lost I found but late—
And must I now forgo it again?
Why must I meet it and miss it straight?
My precious pearl has doubled my pain.
What use is treasure in worldly state
If a man must lose it and mourn in vain?
Now little I reck what trials remain,
What bitter exile and banishment,
For Fortune is bound to be my bane
And suffer I must by her consent."

4

"Such dire presentiments of distress,"
Said she, "I cannot comprehend;
But grief for a loss that matters less
Makes many miss what might amend.
Better to cross yourself, and bless
The name of the Lord, whatever he send;
No good can come of your willfulness;
Who bears bad luck must learn to bend.
Though like a stricken doe, my friend,
You plunge and bray, with loud lament,
This way and that, yet in the end
As he decrees, you must consent.

5

"Dissent, indict him through the years,
His step stirs not one inch astray.
No tittle is gained for all your tears,
Though you should grieve and never be gay.
Abate your bluster, be not so fierce,
And seek his grace as soon as you may,
For prayer has power to bite and pierce
And call compassion into play.
His mercy can wipe your tears away,
Redeem your loss, restore content,
But, grudge or be glad, agree or gainsay,
All lies with him to give consent."

VII

1

Then I assented, answering in dread,
"Let not my Lord be wrathful here
Though blindly I rave, with speech ill-sped;
Mourning had made me mad, or near.
As water flows from a fountainhead
I cast myself in his mercy clear;
Heap no reproaches on my head
Though I should stray, my dearest dear,
But speak in charity and good cheer;
Be merciful, remembering this:
You gave me a heavy grief to bear,
Who once were ground of all my bliss.

2

"My bliss you have been and bitterest woe;
The grief was the greater as time ran on;
Since last I looked for you high and low
I could not tell where my pearl had gone.
I rejoice in it now as long ago,
And when we parted we were as one;
God forbid I should vex you so—
We meet so seldom at any milestone.
Your courtesy is second to none;
I am of earth, and speak amiss,
But the mercy of Christ and Mary and John,
These are the ground of all my bliss.

3

"I see you set in bliss profound,
And I afflicted, felled by fate;
And little you care though I am bound
To suffer harm and hardship great;
But since we are met upon this ground
I would beseech, without debate,
That in sober speech you would expound
The life you lead both early and late.
Indeed, I am glad that your estate
Is raised to such honor and worthiness;
It is my joy to contemplate
And royal road of all my bliss."

4

"Now bliss befall you!" she replied
In form and feature that had no peer,
"And welcome here to walk and bide;

Such words are grateful to my ear.
Headstrong hearts and arrogant pride,
I tell you, are wholly detested here;
My Lord the Lamb is loath to chide,
For all are meek who behold him near.
And when in his house you shall appear,
Be wholly devout in humbleness,
For that delights my Lord so dear
That is the ground of all my bliss.

5

"A blissful life I lead, you say;
You ask in what station I reside;
You know when pearl first slipped away
I was tender of age, by time untried.
But my Lord the Lamb whom all obey,
He took me to him to be his bride,
Crowned me queen in bliss to stay,
Forever and ever glorified.
And seized of his heritage far and wide
Am I, his love, being wholly his;
His royal rank, his praise, his pride
Are root and ground of all my bliss."

VIII

1

"Oh, blissful one, can this be right?"
Said I, "Forgive me if I should err;
Are you the queen of heaven's height
Whom we in this world must all revere?
We believe in Mary, a virgin bright,
Who bore to man God's Son so dear;
Now who could assume her crown, by right,
But she in some feature fairer were?
Yet as none is lovely like unto her,
We call her Phoenix of Araby,
Sent flawless from the artificer
As was our Queen of courtesy."

2

"Courteous Queen!" that blithe one said
Kneeling to ground with upturned face,
"Matchless Mother, most lovely Maid,
Blessed beginner of every grace!"
Then rose she up, and silent stayed,
And spoke to me across that space:
"Sir, gifts are gained here, and prizes paid,
But none on another presumes or preys.

Empress peerless ever to praise
Of heaven and earth and hell is she,
Yet puts no man from his rightful place,
For she is Queen of courtesy.

3

"The court of the kingdom whose crown I bear
Has a property by nature and name:
Each who gains admittance there
Is king of that realm, or queen of the same,
And none would lessen the others' share
But each one, glad of the others' fame,
Would wish their crowns five times as fair,
Had they the power of amending them;
But she who bore Jesu in Bethlehem
Over all of us here has sovereignty,
And none of our number carps at that claim,
For she is Queen of courtesy.

4

"By courtesy, so says St. Paul,[3]
We are members of Christ in joy profound,
As head, arms, legs, and navel and all
Are parts of one person hale and sound;
Likewise each Christian soul I call
A loyal limb of the Lord renowned;
Now what dispute could ever befall
Between two limbs in a body bound?
Though hand or wrist bear a golden round,
Your head will never the sorrier be:
Just so in love is each of us crowned
A king or queen by courtesy."

5

"Courtesy, no doubt, there is,
And charity rife your ranks among;
Yet truly—take it not amiss—
I cannot but think your words are wrong.
You set yourself too high in this,
To be crowned a queen, that was so young;
Why, what more honor might be his
That had lived in hardship late and long
And suffered pains and penance strong
To purchase bliss in heaven on high?
How might he more have thriven in throng
Than be crowned a king by courtesy?

3. I Corinthians 12:12–21, 26–27.

IX

1

"That courtesy too free appears
If all be true as you portray;
You lived in our country not two years—
You could not please the Lord, or pray,
Or say 'Our Father,' or Creed rehearse—
And crowned a queen the very first day!
I cannot well believe my ears,
That God could go so far astray.
The style of countess, so I would say,
Were fair enough to attain unto,
Or a lesser rank in heaven's array,
But a queen! It is beyond your due."

2

"Beyond all due his bounty flows,"
So answered she in words benign;
"For all is justice that he does,
And truth is in his each design.
As the tale in the Gospel of Matthew goes
In the mass that blesses the bread and wine,
In parable his words propose
A likeness to the realm divine.[4]
A man possessed a vineyard fine—
So runs the tale in sermon true—
The time was come to tend the vine
By tasks assigned in order due.

3

"The laborers duly gathered round;
The lord rose up by daybreak bright,
Sought at the market-place, and found
Some who would serve his turn aright.
By the same bargain each was bound:
Let a penny a day his pains requite;
Then forth they go into his ground
And prune and bind and put things right.
He went back late by morning light,
Found idle fellows not a few;
'Why stand you idle here in sight?
Has not this day its service due?'

4

" 'Duly we came ere break of day,'
So answered they in unison;

4. Matthew 20:1–16.

'The sun has risen and here we stay
And look for labor and yet find none.'
'Go to the vine; do what you may,'
So said the lord, 'till day is done;
Promptly at nightfall I shall pay
Such hire as each by right has won.'
So at the vine they labored on,
And still the lord, the long day through,
Brought in new workmen one by one
Till dusk approached at season due.

5

"When time was due of evensong,
The sunset but one hour away,
He saw there idle men in throng
And had these sober words to say:
'Why stand you idle all day long?'
None had required their help, said they.
'Go to the vine, young men and strong,
And do as much there as you may.'
Soon the earth grew dim and grey;
The sun long since had sunk from view;
He summoned them to take their pay;
The day had passed its limit due.

X

1

"Duly the lord, at day's decline,
Said to the steward, 'Sir, proceed;
Pay what I owe this folk of mine;
And lest men chide me here, take heed:
Set them all in a single line,
Give each a penny as agreed;
Start with the last that came to the vine,
And let the first the last succeed.'
And then the first began to plead;
Long had they toiled, they said and swore;
'These in an hour had done their deed;
It seems to us we should have more.

2

" 'More have we served, who suffered through
The heat of the day till evening came,
Than these who stayed but an hour or two,
Yet you allow them equal claim.'
Then said the lord to one of that crew,
'Friend, I will not change the game;
Take your wage and away with you!

I offered a penny, to all the same;
Why begin to bicker and blame?
Was not our covenant set of yore?
Higher than covenant none should aim;
Why should you then ask for more?

3

" 'More, am I not at liberty
To give my own as I wish to do?
Or have you lifted an evil eye,
As I am good, to none untrue?'
'Thus,' says Christ, 'shall I shift it awry:
The last shall be the first in the queue,
And the first the last, were he never so spry,
For many are called, but friends are few.'
So poor men take their portion too,
Though late they came and puny they were,
And though they make but little ado,
The mercy of God is much the more.

4

"More of ladyship here is mine,
Of life in flower and never to fade,
Than any man in the world could win
By right and right alone," she said.
"Although but late I began in the vine—
I came at evening, as Fortune bade—
The lord allowed me first in the line
And then and there I was fully paid.
There were others came early and later stayed,
Who labored long and sweated sore,
And still their payment is delayed,
Shall be, perhaps, for many years more."

5

Then with more discourse I demurred:
"There seems small reason in this narration:
God's justice carries across the board
Or Holy Writ is prevarication!
In the psalter of David there stands a word
Admits no cavil or disputation:[5]
'You render to each his just reward,
O ruler of every dispensation!'
Now he who all day kept his station,
If you to payment come in before,
Then the less, the more remuneration,
And ever alike, the less, the more."

5. Psalms 62 (61):12.

XI

1

"Of more and less," she answered straight,
"In the Kingdom of God, no risk obtains,
For each is paid at the selfsame rate
No matter how little or great his gains.
No niggard is our chief of state,
Be it soft or harsh his will ordains;
His gifts gush forth like a spring in spate
Or a stream in a gulley that runs in rains.
His portion is large whose prayers and pains
Please him who rescues when sinners call.
No bliss in heaven but he attains:
The grace of God is enough for all.

2

"Yet for all that, you stubbornly strive
To prove I have taken too great a fee;
You say I, the last to arrive,
Am not worthy so high degree.
When was there ever a man alive,
Were none so pious and pure as he,
Who by some transgression did not contrive
To forfeit the bliss of eternity?
And the older, the oftener the case must be
That he lapsed into sins both great and small.
Then mercy and grace must second his plea:
The grace of God is enough for all.

3

"But grace enough have the innocent:
When first they see the light of day
To the water of baptism they are sent
And brought to the vine without delay.
At once the light, its splendor spent,
Bows down to darkness and decay;
They had done no harm ere home they went;
From the Master's hands they take their pay.
Why should he not acknowledge them, pray?
They were there with the rest, they came at his call—
Yes, and give them their hire straightway:
The grace of God is enough for all.

4

"It is well enough known, the human race
Was formed to live in pure delight.
Our first forefather altered that case

By an apple of which he took a bite.
We all were damned by that disgrace
To die in sorrow and desperate plight
And then in hell to take our place
And dwell there lost in eternal night.[6]
But then there came a remedy right:
Rich blood ran down rood-tree tall
And with it flowed forth water bright:
The grace of God was enough for all.[7]

5

"Enough for all flowed from that well,
Blood and water plain to behold:
By the blood our souls were saved from hell
And the second death decreed of old.[8]
The water is baptism, truth to tell,
That followed the spearhead keen and cold,
Old Adam's deadly guilt to dispel
That swamped us in sins a thousandfold.
Now all is withdrawn that ever could hold
Mankind from bliss, since Adam's fall,
And that was redeemed at a time foretold
And the grace of God is enough for all.

XII

1

"Grace enough that man can have
Who is penitent, having sinned anew,
If with sorrow at heart he cry and crave
And perform the penance that must ensue.
But by right reason, that cannot rave,
The innocent ever receives his due:
To punish the guiltless with the knave
Is a plan God never was party to.
The guilty, by contrition true,
Can attain to mercy requisite,
But he that never had guile in view,
The innocent is safe and right.

2

"I know right reason in this case
And thereto cite authority:
The righteous man shall see his face
And the innocent bear him company.
So in a verse the psalter says,[9]

6. Genesis 3:17–19; Matthew 13:41–42;   8. Revelation 20:14.
Romans 5:12.   9. Psalms 24 (23):3–4.
7. John 19:34; Ephesians 1:3–7.

'Lord, who shall climb your hill on high
Or rest within your holy place?'
And readily then he makes reply:
'Hands that did no injury,
Heart that was always pure and light:
There shall his steps be stayed in joy';
The innocent ever is safe by right.

3

"The righteous also in due time,
He shall approach that noble tor,
Who cozens his neighbor with no crime
Nor wastes his life in sin impure.
King Solomon tells in text sublime
Of Wisdom and her honored lore;[1]
By narrow ways she guided him
And lo! God's kingdom lay before.
As who should say, 'Yon distant shore—
Win it you may ere fall of night
If you make haste'; but evermore
The innocent ever is safe by right.

4

"Of the righteous man I find report
In the psalter of David, if ever you spied it:[2]
'Call not your servant, Lord, to court,
For judgment is grim if justice guide it.'
And when to that seat you must resort
Where each man's case shall be decided,
Claim the right, you may be caught short.
By this same proof I have provided.
But he who, scourged and sore derided,
Bled on the cross through mortal spite,
Grant that your sentence be decided
By innocence and not by right.

5

"Who reads the Book of rightful fame
May learn of it infallibly
How good folk with their children came
To Jesus walking in Galilee.[3]
The touch of his hand they sought for them
For the goodness in him plain to see;
The disciples banned that deed with blame
And bade the children let him be.
But Jesus gathered them round his knee
And of that reprimand made light;

---

1. Wisdom (Apocrypha) 10:9–10.
2. Psalms 143 (142):2.

3. Mark 10:13–16; Luke 18:15–17.

'Of such is the kingdom of heaven,' said he;
The innocent ever is safe by right.

XIII

1

"Jesus on his faithful smiled
And said, 'God's kingdom shall be won
By him who seeks it as a child,
For other entry-right is none.'
Harmless, steadfast, undefiled,
Unsullied bright to gaze upon,
When such stand knocking, meek and mild,
Straightway the gate shall be undone.
There is the endless bliss begun
That the jeweler sought in earthly estate
And sold all his goods, both woven and spun,
To purchase a pearl immaculate.[4]

2

"This immaculate pearl I tell you of,
The jeweler gave his wealth to gain,
Is like the realm of heaven above;
The Father of all things said it plain.
No spot it bears, nor blemish rough,
But blithe in rondure ever to reign,
And of righteousness it is prize and proof:
Lo, here on my breast it long has lain;
Bestowed by the Lamb so cruelly slain,
His peace to betoken and designate;
I bid you turn from the world insane
And purchase your pearl immaculate."

3

"Immaculate pearl whom white pearls crown,
Who bear," said I, "the pearl of price,
Who fashioned your form? Who made your gown?
Oh, he that wrought it was most wise!
Such beauty in nature never was known;
Pygmalion never painted your eyes,
Nor Aristotle, of long renown,
Discoursed of these wondrous properties,
Your gracious aspect, your angel guise,
More white than the lily, and delicate:
What duties high, what dignities
Are marked by the pearl immaculate?"

4. Matthew 13:45–46.

4

"My immaculate Lamb, my destiny sweet,"
Said she, "who can all harm repair,
He made me his mate in marriage meet,
Though once such a match unfitting were.
When I left your world of rain and sleet
He called me in joy to join him there:
'Come hither, my dove without deceit,
For you are spotless, past compare.'[5]
He gave me strength, he made me fair,
He crowned me a virgin consecrate,
And washed in his blood these robes I wear,[6]
And clad me in pearls immaculate."

5

"Immaculate being, bright as flame,
In royalties set and sanctified,
Tell me now, what is that Lamb
That sought you out to become his bride?
Over all others you pressed your claim
To live in honor with him allied,
Yet many a noble and worthy dame
For Christ's dear sake has suffered and died;
And you have thrust those others aside
And reserved for yourself that nuptial state,
Yourself all alone, so big with pride,
A matchless maid and immaculate?"

XIV

1

"Immaculate," came her answer clear,
"Unblemished am I, my peers among;
So much I claim with honor here,
But matchless—there you have it wrong.
We all are brides of the Lamb so dear,
One hundred and forty-four thousand strong,
In Apocalypse the words appear
As John beheld it and told with tongue.[7]
Thousands on thousands, virgins young,
He saw on Mount Sion in sacred dream,
Arrayed for the wedding in comely throng
In the city called New Jerusalem.

2

"Of Jerusalem I speak perforce,
To tell his nature and degree,

---

5. Song of Solomon 4:7; 5:2.   7. Revelation 14:1.
6. Revelation 7:13–14.

My jewel dear, my joy's sole source,
My Lamb, my lord, my love, all three.
In the prophet Isaiah we find discourse
Of him and his humility,[8]
Condemned and martyred without remorse
And on false charges of felony,
As a sheep to the slaughter led was he,
As a lamb to the shearers meek and tame;
His lips were sealed to all inquiry
When Jews were his judge in Jerusalem.

3

"In Jerusalem my true love died,
Rent by rude hands with pain and woe;
Freely he perished for our pride,
And suffered our doom in mortal throe.[9]
His blessèd face, or ever he died,
Was made to bleed by many a blow;[1]
For sin he set his power aside
Though never he sinned who suffered so.
For us he was beaten and bowed low
And racked on the rood-tree rough and grim,
And meek as the lamb with fleece of snow
He breathed his last in Jerusalem.

4

"In Jerusalem, Jordan, and Galilee,
When John the Baptist preached abroad,
The words with Isaiah well agree
That he said when Jesus before him stood;[2]
He made of him this prophecy:
'Steadfast as stone, O Lamb of God,
Who takes away the iniquity
That all this world has wrought in blood';
And he was guiltless and ever good,
Yet bore our sins and atoned for them;
O who can reckon his parenthood
Who perished for us in Jerusalem?

5

"In Jerusalem my lover true
Appeared as a lamb of purest white
In the eyes of the prophets old and new
For his meek mien and piteous plight.
The third fits well with the other two,
In Revelation written aright;[3]

8. Isaiah 53:7, 9.
9. Isaiah 53:4–5.
1. Matthew 26:67.

2. John 1:29.
3. Revelation 5:1, 6–7.

Where the saints sat round in retinue
The Apostle saw him throned in light,
Bearing the book with pages bright
And the seven seals set round the rim,
And all hosts trembled at that sight,
In hell, in earth, and Jerusalem.

XV

1

"This Jerusalem Lamb in his array
Was whiter far than tongue could tell;
No spot or speck might on him stay,
His fair rich fleece did so excel.
And so each sinless soul, I say,
Is a worthy wife with the Lamb to dwell,
And though he fetch a score each day
No strife is stirred in our citadel,
But would each brought four others as well—
The more the merrier in blessedness!
Our love is increased as our numbers swell,
And honor more and never the less.

2

"Less of bliss none brings us here
Who bear the pearl upon our breast;
No mark of strife could ever appear
Where the precious pearl is worn for crest.
Our bodies lie on earthen bier,
And you go grieving, sore distressed,
But we, with knowledge full and clear,
See in one death all wrong redressed.
The Lamb has laid our cares to rest;
We partake of his table in joyfulness;
Each one's share of bliss is best.
Nor ever in honor any the less.

3

"Lest less you believe, incline your ear
To the Book of Revelation true:[4]
'I saw,' says John, 'the Lamb appear
On the Mount of Sion, all white of hue,
With a hundred thousand maidens dear
And forty-four thousand more in view;
On all their foreheads written were
The name of the Lamb, of his Father too.
But then in heaven a clamor grew,
Like waters running in rapid race;

4. **Revelation** 14:1–5.

As thunder crashes in storm-cloud blue,
Such was that sound, and nothing less.

4

" 'Nevertheless, though it shouted shrill
And made the heavens resound again,
I heard them sing upon that hill
A new song, a most noble strain;
As harpers touch their harps with skill
Their voices lifted, full and plain;
And well they followed with a will
The phrases of that fair refrain.
Before his throne who ever shall reign
And the four beasts ranged about the dais
And the solemn elders of that domain,
Great was their song, and grew no less.

5

" 'Nevertheless, there was none had might
Or for all his art might ever aspire
To sing that song, save those in white
Who follow the Lamb their lord and sire;
For they are redeemed from earth's dark night
As first fruits given to God entire,
And joined with the Lamb on Sion's height,
As like himself in speech and attire,
For never, in deed or heart's desire,
Their tongues were touched with untruthfulness;
And none can sever that sinless choir
From that master immaculate, nevertheless.' "

6

"Never less welcome let me find,"
Said I, "for the queries I propose;
I should not tempt your noble mind
Whom Christ the Lord to his chamber chose.
I am of mire and mere mankind,
And you so rich and rare a rose,
And here to eternal bliss assigned
Where joy fails not, but forever grows.
Now, dame, whom simplicity's self endows,
I would beseech a favor express,
And though I am rough and rude, God knows,
Let it be granted nevertheless.

XVI

1

"Nevertheless, if you can see
In my request a reason sound,
Deny not my dejected plea,
But where grace is, let grace abound.
Have you no hall, no hostelry,
To dwell in and meet in daily round?
You tell of Jerusalem rich and free
Where reigned King David the renowned,
But that cannot be near this ground
But lies in Judea, by reckoning right;
As you under moon are flawless found,
Your lodgings should be wholly bright.

2

"These holy virgins in radiant guise,
By thousands thronged in processional—
That city must be of uncommon size
That keeps you together, one and all.
It were not fit such jewels of price
Should lie unsheltered by roof or wall,
Yet where these river-banks arise
I see no building large or small.
Beside this stream celestial
You linger alone, none else in sight;
If you have another house or hall,
Show me that dwelling wholly bright."

3

That wholly blissful, that spice heaven-sent,
Declared, "In Judea's fair demesne
The city lies, where the Lamb once went
To suffer for man death's anguish keen.
The old Jerusalem by that is meant,
For there the old guilt was canceled clean,
But the new, in vision prescient,
John saw sent down from God pristine.[5]
The spotless Lamb of gracious mien
Has carried us all to that fair site,
And as in his flock no fleck is seen,
His hallowed halls are wholly bright.

4

"Two holy cities I figure forth;
One name suits well with both of these,

5. Revelation 21:2.

Which in the language of your birth
Is 'City of God,' or 'Sight of Peace.'[6]
In the one the Lamb brought peace on earth
Who suffered for our iniquities;
In the other is peace with heavenly mirth,
And ever to last, and never to cease.
And to that city in glad release
From fleshly decay our souls take flight;
There glory and bliss shall ever increase
In the household that is wholly bright."

5

"Holy maid compassionate,"
Said I to that fresh flower and gay,
"Let me approach those ramparts great
And see the chamber where you stay."
"The Lord forbids," she answered straight,
"That a stranger in his streets should stray,
But through the Lamb enthroned in state
I have won you a sight of it this day.
Behold it from far off you may,
But no man's foot may there alight;
You have no power to walk that way
Save as a spirit wholly bright.

XVII

1

"This holy city that I may show,
Walk upwards toward the river's head,
And here against you I shall go
Until to a hill your path has led."
Then to stir I was not slow,
But under leafy boughs I sped
Until from a hill I looked below
And saw the city, as she had said,
Beyond the stream in splendor spread,
That brighter than shafts of sunlight shone.
In Apocalypse it may all be read
As he set it forth, the apostle John.[7]

2

As John the apostle saw it of old
I saw the city beyond the stream,
Jerusalem the new and fair to behold,
Sent down from heaven by power supreme.
The streets were paved with precious gold,
As flawless pure as glass agleam,

6. Revelation 3:12; Ezekiel 13:16.   7. Revelation 21:10–27; 22:1–2.

Based on bright gems of worth untold,
Foundation-stones twelvefold in team;
And set in series without a seam,
Each level was a single stone,
As he beheld it in sacred dream
In Apocalypse, the apostle John.

3

As John had named them in writ divine
Each stone in order by name I knew;
Jasper was the first in line;
At the lowest level it came in view;
Green ingrained I saw it shine.
The second was the sapphire blue;
The clear chalcedony, rare and fine,
Was third in degree in order due.
The fourth the emerald green of hue;
Sardonyx fifth was set thereon;
The sixth the ruby he saw ensue
In Apocalypse, the apostle John.

4

To these John joined the chrysolite,
The seventh in that foundation's face;
The eighth the beryl clear and white,
The twin-hued topaz ninth to trace;
The chrysoprase tenth in order right;
Jacinth held the eleventh place;
The twelfth, the amethyst most of might,
Blent blue and purple in royal blaze.
The jasper walls above that base
Like lustrous glass to gaze upon;
I knew them all by his every phrase
In Apocalypse, the apostle John.

5

As John had written, so I was ware
How broad and steep was each great tier;
As long as broad as high foursquare
The city towered on twelvefold pier.
The streets like glass in brilliance bare,
The walls like sheen on parchment sheer;
The dwellings all with gemstones rare
Arrayed in radiance far and near.
The sides of that perimeter
Twelve thousand furlongs spanned, each one;
Length, breadth, and height were measured there
Before his eyes, the apostle John.

XVIII

1

Yet more, John saw on every side
Three gateways set commensurate,
So twelve I counted in compass wide,
The portals rich with precious plate.
Each gate a pearl of princely pride,
Unfading, past all earthly fate,
On which a name was signified
Of Israel's sons, in order of date,
That is, by birthright ranked in state,
The eldest ever the foremost one.
The streets were alight both early and late;
They needed neither sun nor moon.

2

Sun and moon were far surpassed;
The Lord was their lamp eternally,
The Lamb their lantern ever to last
Made bright that seat of sovereignty.
Through roof and wall my looking passed,
Pure substance hindered not to see;
There I beheld the throne steadfast
With the emblems that about it be,
As John in text gave testimony;
Upon it sat the Lord triune;
A river therefrom ran fresh and free,
More bright by far than sun or moon.

3

Sun nor moon shone never so fair
As that flood of plenteous waters pure;
Full it flowed in each thoroughfare;
No filth or taint its brightness bore.
Church they had none, nor chapel there,
House of worship, nor need therefor;
The Almighty was their place of prayer,
The Lamb the sacrifice all to restore.
No lock was set on gate or door
But evermore open both night and noon;
None may take refuge on that floor
Who bears any spot beneath the moon.

4

The moon has in that reign no right;
Too spotty she is, of body austere;
And they who dwell there know no night—

Of what avail her varying sphere?
And set beside that wondrous light
That shines upon the waters clear
The planets would lose their lustre quite,
And the sun itself would pale appear.
Beside the river are trees that bear
Twelve fruits of life their boughs upon;
Twelve times a year they burgeon there
And renew themselves with every moon.

5

Beneath the moon so much amazed
No fleshly heart could bear to be
As by that city on which I gazed,
Its form so wondrous was to see.
As a quail that couches, dumb and dazed,
I stared on that great symmetry;
Nor rest nor travail my soul could taste,
Pure radiance so had ravished me.
For this I say with certainty:
Had a man in the body borne that boon,
No doctor's art, for fame or fee,
Had saved his life beneath the moon.

XIX

1

As the great moon begins to shine
While lingers still the light of day,
So in those ramparts crystalline
I saw a procession wend its way.
Without a summons, without a sign,
The city was full in vast array
Of maidens in such raiment fine
As my blissful one had worn that day.
As she was crowned, so crowned were they;
Adorned with pearls, in garments white;
And in like fashion, gleaming gay,
They bore the pearl of great delight.

2

With great delight, serene and slow,
They moved through every golden street;
Thousands on thousands, row on row,
All in one raiment shining sweet.
Who gladdest looked, was hard to know;
The Lamb led on at station meet,
Seven horns of gold upon his brow,[8]

8. Revelation 5:6.

His robe like pearls with rays replete.
Soon they approached God's mighty seat;
Though thick in throng, unhurried quite;
As maidens at communion meet
They moved along with great delight.

3

Delight that at his coming grew
Was greater than my tongue can tell;
The elders when he came in view
Prostrate as one before him fell;
Hosts of angels in retinue
Cast incense forth of sweetest smell;
Then all in concert praised anew
That jewel with whom in joy they dwell.[9]
The sound could pierce through the earth to hell
When the powers of heaven in song unite;
To share his praises in citadel
My heart indeed had great delight.

4

Delight and wonder filled me in flood
To hear all heaven the Lamb acclaim;
Gladdest he was, most kind and good
Of any that ever was known to fame.
His dress so white, so mild his mood,
His looks so gracious, himself the same;
But a wound there was, and wide it stood,
Thrust near his heart with deadly aim.
Down his white side the red blood came;
"O God," thought I, "who had such spite?
A breast should consume with sorrow and shame
Ere in such deeds it took delight."

5

The Lamb's delight was clearly seen;
Though a bitter wound he had to bear,
His countenance shone no less serene,
So glorious bright his glances were.
I looked where that great host had been,
Crowned all with life in radiance clear;
And then I saw my little queen
That I thought but now I had stood so near.
Lord! how she laughed and made good cheer
Among her friends, who was so white!
To rush in the river then and there
I longed with love and great delight.

9. Revelation 5:8, 11–14.

XX

1

Moved by delight of sight and sound,
My maddened mind all fate defied.
I would follow her there, my newly found,
Beyond the river though she must bide.
I thought that nothing could turn me round,
Forestall me, or stop me in mid-stride,
And wade I would from the nearer ground
And breast the stream, though I sank and died.
But soon those thoughts were thrust aside;
As I made for the river incontinent
I was summoned away and my wish denied:
My Prince therewith was not content.

2

It contented him not that I, distraught,
Should dare the river that rimmed the glade;
Though reckless I was, and overwrought,
In a moment's space my steps were stayed.
For just as I started from the spot
I was reft of my dream and left dismayed;
I waked in that same garden-plot,
On that same mound my head was laid.
I stretched my hand where Pearl had strayed;
Great fear befell me, and wonderment;
And, sighing, to myself I said,
"Let all things be to his content."

3

I was ill content to be dispossessed
Of the sight of her that had no peer
Amid those scenes so bright and blessed;
Such longing seized me, I swooned, or near;
Then sorrow broke from my burning breast;
"O honored Pearl," I said, "how dear
Was your every word and wise behest
In this true vision vouchsafed me here.
If you in a garland never sere
Are set by that Prince all-provident,
Then happy am I in dungeon drear
That he with you is well content."

4

Had I but sought to content my Lord
And taken his gifts without regret,
And held my place and heeded the word

Of the noble Pearl so strangely met,
Drawn heavenward by divine accord
I had seen and heard more mysteries yet;
But always men would have and hoard
And gain the more, the more they get.
So banished I was, by cares beset,
From realms eternal untimely sent;
How madly, Lord, they strive and fret
Whose acts accord not with your content!

5

To content that Prince and well agree,
Good Christians can with ease incline,
For day and night he has proved to be
A Lord, a God, a friend benign.
These words came over the mound to me
As I mourned my Pearl so flawless fine,
And to God committed her full and free,
With Christ's dear blessing bestowing mine,
As in the form of bread and wine
Is shown us daily in sacrament;
O may we serve him well, and shine
As precious pearls to his content.

Amen.

The Metrical Form

Pearl is written in a line of four metrical units in which "chief syllables" (those recurring at what are felt as commensurate intervals of time) alternate with "intermediate syllables"—usually one, sometimes two. The meter may be described in more traditional terms as iambic tetrameter varied by an occasional anapest, but it exhibits a higher degree of correspondence between abstract metrical patterns and natural patterns of stress than the iambic meters of classical English poetry. Sequences of strong chief syllables alternating with weak intermediate syllables are predominant; the strong, even "beat" set up by these tends in turn to impose itself (though not to the point of distortion) on sequences in which such alternation is less marked. The difference is one of degree. The meter of *Pearl* is more like musical rhythm than that of the traditional iambic line, though no ryhthms constituted by words alone can be as temporally regular as music unless the words are artificially chanted. Consider the following well-known passage from Robert Frost's "Stopping by Woods on a Snowy Evening":

> My little horse must think it queer
> To stop without a farmhouse near
> Between the woods and frozen lake
> The darkest evening of the year.

Translated into the meter of *Pearl*, it might run thus:

> My horse in harness must think it queer
> To stop with never a farmhouse near
> 'Twixt wintry woods and frozen lake
> On the darkest night of all the year.

What makes the difference? To begin with, a syllable has been added to three of Frost's lines to make an "irregular" anapestic foot: "-ness must think" in line 1, "-er a farm" in line 2, "on the dark-" in line 4. But this in itself would not have greatly changed the movement of the verse. A more important alteration is the rewording of the lines to make chief syllables uniformly strong. In the original, three prepositions, *without*, *between*, and, most important, *of*, occupy chief position. Since prepositions normally receive less stress than nouns and other important carriers of meaning, the lines in which these words appear have one weak foot, and by a natural principle in language, they also run faster. In the altered stanza, prepositions are demoted to intermediate rank. The predominance of chief over intermediate syllables is enhanced by alliterative linkings which make them stand out even more: between *horse* and *harness*, *wintry* and *woods*, and, less perceptibly, *never* and *near*. Such combinations were the staple of the so-called long alliterative line used by the *Pearl*-poet in *Sir Gawain*, *Purity*, and *Patience*, in which they are a requirement of the form. Rhyme takes the place of alliteration as a formal device in *Pearl*, but though alliteration is not a necessary constituent of the verse, there is a great deal of it. The

poet seems to have considered it a desirable ornament, especially in emo-
tionally charged passages of invocation or description such as are found in
sections XIII and XVII.

The meter of *Pearl* is strong and easy to feel. It has affinities with musical
rhythm, as has been said, and with ballads, nursery rhymes, and other popu-
lar forms of poetry as well. If we look for something like it in modern liter-
ature, we will find it in Gerard Manley Hopkins, whose "sprung rhythm"
helped to free the traditional iambic line from syllabic constraints:

> This darksome burn, horseback brown,
> His rollrock highroad roaring down,
> In coop and in comb the fleece of his foam
> Flutes and low to the lake falls home.

These four-stress lines from "Inversnaid" have many of the characteristics
of the meter of *Pearl*. Chief position is uniformly occupied by strongly
stressed syllables, and the iambic movement is varied by three anapests,
"and in comb" and "of his foam" in line 3 and "to the lake" in line 4.
Important words are linked by alliteration: *coop* and *comb*, *fleece* and
foam, *low* and *lake*, among others. The only significant difference is that
Hopkins' lines are heavier. A number of intermediate syllables receive a
degree of stress close to that given chief syllables; a sequence like "rollrock
highroad" is not found in *Pearl*.

That the meter of *Pearl* has these general features seems clear enough,
but there is disagreement about some of the details, particularly as regards
the pronunciation of unstressed syllables. A comparison with Chaucer, who
also wrote in the late fourteenth century and whose metrical practices are
well understood, will be helpful here.

The *Pearl*-poet seems to follow a metrical convention forbidding the
omission of intermediate syllables within the line except under certain
specified conditions. Two chief syllables do not occur side by side except
when the first one is followed by a pause, usually in mid-line. In that case
the second one is regularly followed by two intermediate syllables, so that
these and the chief syllable which follows them make up an anapestic foot.
Using c for chief syllables, x for intermediate syllables, and / for a pause,
we can express the resultant pattern schematically as (x) c x c / c x x c.
In relation to the basic pattern (x) c x c x c x c, the fifth and sixth syllables
of such a line form a "reversed foot" of the sort familiar to students of
Chaucerian and later English verse; the same substitution of c x for x c
occurs frequently at the beginning of the line as well. The second of the
following two lines from *Pearl*,

> c x   c   x   c   x c
> "Cortayse Quen," thenne sayde that gaye,
> c x   x c   c   x   x c
> Knelande to grounde, folde up hyr face,   (VIII, 2)

has reversed feet in both initial and medial position.

It follows that the patterns x c c x c x c and x c x c x c c, among others,
ought not to occur. Where they seem to be present, as in the line

> x c   x   c   x c   c
> That dotz bot thrych my hert thrange,   (I, 2)

it is possible to appeal from the form of a word as we find it spelled in the manuscript to its form at an earlier stage of the history of the language and in Chaucer's verse. *Hert* "heart" is derived from Old English *heorte*; it is spelled *herte* in the best Chaucerian manuscripts, and there are many lines in Chaucer in which a disyllabic pronunciation *hertë* is obviously called for. The word is also spelled *herte* several times in *Pearl*; sounding of *-e* is implied by the meter in at least one such case:

x   x   c   x c   x   c x   c x
The more strengthe of joye myn herte straynez.   (III, 1)

It seems legitimate to conclude that in the line "That dotz bot thrych my hert thrange" the poet originally wrote *herte*; the scribe who copied out the poem has omitted the final *-e*. Much more evidence of the same sort can be gathered to show that final *-e* is sounded sporadically throughout *Pearl*, as in Chaucer, to avoid the omission of an intermediate syllable without a compensating "reversed foot," and that *-e* in such cases can be assumed to have been present in the lines as the poet originally wrote them, whether or not it is reproduced in the single copy that has come down to us. Some metrically based emendations will be found in the specimen scansions below.

But a comparison of *Pearl* with Chaucer reveals important differences as well as similarities. There are at least two lines in which the metrical evidence clearly indicates that *herte* is monosyllabic; the word is spelled *herte* in one, *hert* in the other: "For urthely herte myght not suffyse" (III, 2), and "That stong myn hert ful stray atount" (III, 5). Here the poet is using the more modern form, and the proportion of such forms to the older forms with sounded *-e* in his verse is considerably greater than it is in Chaucer. The *Pearl*-poet also differs radically from Chaucer in his treatment of *-e* in rhyming words. Whereas Chaucer regularly rhymes words ending in *-e* with other words ending in *-e* (the implication being that we are to pronounce *-e* in both), the *Pearl*-poet rhymes words that have, or originally had, *-e* with words that do not. Thus, Chaucer rhymes *face*, *place*, and *space*, from French *facë*, *placë*, and *espacë*, respectively; the *Pearl*-poet also rhymes these words, but with them he combines *was* (Old English *waes*) and *case* (Old French *cas*), as Chaucer does not do. The implication is that *-e* is not pronounced in rhyme-words in *Pearl*, even when it is present in all the members of a rhyming group.

It thus appears that the metrical patterns of *Pearl* reflect a more "modern" state of the language than Chaucer's verse does, even though Chaucer and the *Pearl*-poet were contemporaries, and this accords with what historians of the language have to tell us: Chaucer's London English was conservative as compared to that of the northwest Midlands, where the *Pearl*-poet presumably lived. It is also likely that Chaucer himself used obsolescent modes of pronunciation to make his meter. Forms like *hertë* would certainly seem to have been literary archaisms for the *Pearl*-poet, historically valid because handed down from one generation of poets to another, but no longer current in the spoken language.

The four-part line in *Pearl* is itself one element in a series of progressively larger patterns, beginning with the three four-line sections of the twelve-line stanza. Sections and stanzas alike are marked off, whether for the external ear of the listener or the inner ear of the reader, by rhyme, syntactic division, and repetition. There is almost no enjambment or running over of syntax from line to line; most lines end in a pause of at least comma strength, with a semicolon or period at the end of every group of four, and a period at the end of every stanza or verse-paragraph. The second and fourth occurrences of the b-rhyme signalize the end of the first two sections of each stanza, and a pivotal repetition of the b-rhyme occurs in two adjoining lines as the pattern abab shifts to bcbc. The second c-rhyme is also the link-word of each section, and a change in this word marks the transition from each five-stanza section to the next.

The total effect, as the poem is heard or read in its entirety, is powerfully cumulative. The shift from link-word to link-word measures off in stages the rise in intensity of rhetoric and feeling, from the time of the introduction of the parable of the heavenly pearl in section XII until the dreamer rushes toward the stream at the beginning of section XX, rather like a series of shifts to the next higher musical key in successive choruses of a popular song. Toward the end, we respond imaginatively to the playing out of the human drama, while recognizing, on the formal level, patterns of recurrence and return. It is a remarkable experience, one which can only be enhanced by our understanding of the elements that combine to bring it about.

Specimen Scansions

To illustrate the metrical patterns of *Pearl*, I have chosen the opening stanza, a stanza from the pearl-maiden's argument immediately following her narration of the parable of the vineyard, and a stanza from the dreamer's vision of the celestial Jerusalem. Each is given in the original and in translation. In transcribing the original, I have substituted *u* for *v* and *v* for *u* in accordance with modern practice, *th* for the Middle English letter *thorn*, *y* for Middle English *yogh* in initial position, *gh* for *yogh* in medial position, and *gh* or *z* for *yogh* in final position, depending on the sound represented. I have used the text of *Pearl* as edited by E. V. Gordon (Oxford, 1953).

The "rules" determining scansions are as described above. The inflectional endings *-ed* (as in *jugged* "judged") and *-ez* (as in *sydez* "sides") had continued to be pronounced as syllables in the language of the *Pearl*-poet, and are often used by him to provide the necessary intermediate syllables within the line. They could also be contracted, as indicated by their presence in lines where their sounding would result in irregular sequences of three intermediate syllables. Where they are followed by a single intermediate syllable, I have left their metrical status indeterminate, though I am inclined to think that they should be contracted in most, if not all, such cases. I have left *-ez* silent in *hondelyngez* in example 2, on the linguistic grounds that in this word it falls after a syllable bearing less than primary stress; cf. the pronunciation indicated by the meter for *planetez* in example 3.

```
            c x    c x     x   c  x  c
(1)    Perle, plesaunte to prynces paye,

        x   c  x  c x   c    x  c
       To clanly clos in golde so clere,

       c    x  c  x    x  c  x x c
       Oute of oryent, I hardyly saye,

        x    c(x) x  c x   x   c x    c
       Ne proved I never her precios pere.

        x  c      x  c x  x  c    x c
       So rounde, so reken in uche araye,

        x   c      c   x  c x    c
       So smal, so smothe her sydez were,

          x   x c x x  c   x   c   x   c
       Quere-so-ever I jugged gemmez gaye,

       x c    x  c    x c  x   c
       I sette hyr sengeley in synglere.

       x  c  x  c    x c x   x   c
       Allas! I leste hyr in on erbere;

          x     c   x  c     x  c  x  c
       Thurgh gresse to grounde hit fro me yot.
```

```
x    c    x  c (x) x  c  x   c
```
I dewyne, fordolked of luf-daungere

```
x    x   c x c    x  c  x    c
```
Of that pryvy perle wythouten spot.

NOTE. In line 1, *perle* was probably pronounced very much like modern English *peril*.

```
c     x x  c  x  c  x  c
```
Pearl, that a prince is well content

```
x  c  x c  x x   c    x  c
```
To give a circle of gold to wear,

```
c   x x c   x  c x c
```
Boldly I say, all orient

```
x     c    x    c x  c   x c
```
Brought forth none precious like to her;

```
x  c   x x  c   x c x  c
```
So comely in every ornament,

```
x  c  x  x  c    x   c    x  c
```
So slender her sides, so smooth they were,

```
c x   x  c    x  c   x   c
```
Ever my mind was bound and bent

```
x  c  x x c    x  c  x  c
```
To set her apart without a peer.

```
x  x  c x  x   c   x c    x  c
```
In a garden of herbs I lost my dear;

```
x     c  x  c    x c x    c
```
Through grass to ground away it shot;

```
x   c  x     x  c x c x  c
```
Now, lovesick, the heavy loss I bear

```
x    x  c x  c    x  c  x   c
```
Of that secret pearl without a spot.

```
       x     c x   c   x c   x  c
```
(2)   "Ryght thus I knaw wel in this cas

```
c   x   x c x  c  x  c
```
Two men to save is god by skylle:

```
x  c    x   c    x  c x c
```
The ryghtwys man schal se hys face,

```
x  c  x  c x   x  c   x   c
```
The harmlez hathel schal com hym tylle.

```
x  c  x  x  c    x c x  c
```
The Sauter hyt satz thus in a pace:

```
c     x  x  c    x  c  x  c
```
'Lorde, quo schal klymbe thy hygh[e] hylle,

```
x (x) c   x  c    x  c x  c
```
Other rest wythinne thy holy place?'

```
x   c  x c   x   x c  x  c
```
Hymself to onsware he is not dylle:

```
     c     x      c       x  c    x c
'Hondelyngez harme that dyt not ille,
```

```
      x c x   c    x       c  x    c
That is of hert bothe clene and lyght,
```

```
     c     x  x    c  x     c x c
Ther schal hys step[e] stable stylle':
```

```
      x c   x x    c x    c   x c
The innosent is ay saf by ryght.
```

NOTES. *Hygh* (6) and *step* (11) have been emended to provide a nec-
essary intermediate syllable; cf. the general discussion of the metrical form,
above. Note the rhyme *cas: face*, evidence that *-e* in *face* is silent as in mod-
ern English.

```
      x    c   x     c x c    x  c
"I know right reason in this case
```

```
     x    c   x c  x    c x c
And thereto cite authority:
```

```
      x c  x      c    x   c x c
The righteous man shall see his face
```

```
     x    x c  x x    c    x    c   x c
And the innocent bear him company.
```

```
      c x  x  c    x   c x  c
So in a verse the psalter says,
```

```
      c      x  x  c    x    c x    c
'Lord, who shall climb your hill on high
```

```
     x   c    x c   x    c x  c
Or rest within your holy place?'
```

```
     x    c x x   c   x  c     x c
And readily then he makes reply:
```

```
      c     x  c   x c  x c
'Hands that did no injury,
```

```
      c     x   x c  x    c x    c
Heart that was always pure and light:
```

```
      c    x  x   c    x  c    x  c
There shall his steps be stayed in joy';
```

```
      x c   x c  x  c    x c
The innocent is safe by right.
```

```
          x   c    x   x c x c    x  c
(3)   The mone may therof acroche no myghte;
```

```
      x   c    x c  x   c x x   c
To spotty ho is, of body to grym,
```

```
     x   c x  c x   c x  c
And also ther is never nyght.
```

```
      c    x    x  c    x  c    x c
What schulde the mone ther compas clym?
```

```
     x    x c x   c    x   c   x c
And to even wyth that worthly lyght
```

```
    x      c(x) x  c    x   c x    c
That schynez upon the brokez brym

     x   c x   x  c  x  c   x  c
The planetez arn in to pouer a plyght

x      x c x  c     x c x  c
And the sel[ve] sunne ful fer to dym.

x c     x   c x x     c  x     c
Aboute that water arn tres ful schym,

     x    c    x   x  c  x   c    x c
That twelve frytez of lyf con bere ful sone;

       c    x    x   c   x  c(x)  x   c
Twelve sythez on yer thay beren ful frym,

x     x c x   c x c    x   c
And renowlez nwe in uche a mone.
```

Note. *Self* (8) has been emended to *selve*, a disyllablic "weak" form permissible following the definite article. Cf. Chaucer's line "Right in that selvë wisë, soth to seyë" (*Troilus* 3.355).

```
    x   c    x c    x  c    x c
The moon has in that reign no right;

   x    c x  x c  x   c x x    c
Too spotty she is, of body austere;

x    c    x   c    x     c   x c
And they who dwell there know no night—

x    c x c   x   c x      c
Of what avail her varying sphere?

x    c  x c    x   c   x   c
And set beside that wondrous light

     x   c   x c    x  c x    c
That shines upon the waters clear

     x  c x   x    c   x   c x c
The planets would lose their lustre quite

x     x c x c   x    c x  c
And the sun itself would pale appear.

x c     x c x x    c    x  c
Beside the river are trees that bear

     c    x   x c   x   c    x c
Twelve fruits of life their boughs upon;

     c   x   x c    x  c x     c
Twelve times a year they burgeon there

x    x c   x  c    x  c  x c
And renew themselves with every moon.
```

Reading Suggestions

Blanch, R. J., ed. *Sir Gawain and Pearl: Critical Essays*. Indiana University Press, 1966.

Boethius. *The Consolation of Philosophy*, trans. Richard Green. Bobbs-Merrill, Library of Liberal Arts, 1962.

Borroff, Marie. *Sir Gawain and the Green Knight: A Stylistic and Metrical Study*, chaps. 5 and 6. Yale University Press, 1962. (The meter of the rhymed lines of *Sir Gawain*.)

De Lorris, Guillaume, and Jean de Meun. *The Romance of the Rose*, trans. Harry W. Robbins, ed. Charles W. Dunn. E. P. Dutton, 1962.

Giamatti, A. Bartlett. *The Earthly Paradise and the Renaissance Epic*, chap. 1. Princeton University Press, 1966.

Kean, Patricia M. *The Pearl: An Interpretation*. Routledge and Kegan Paul, 1967.

Pearl and Sir Gawain and the Green Knight, ed. A. C. Cawley. Everyman's Library, 346. J. M. Dent, 1962. (Original texts with marginal glosses and introductory essay.)

Pearl, ed. E. V. Gordon. Oxford University Press, 1953. (Scholarly edition of the original text.)

Spearing, A. C. *The Gawain-poet: A Critical Study*. Cambridge University Press, 1970. (A chapter on each of the four poems.)